EARLY LEARNING
For three- to five-year-olds

The Parcel

Story by Pie Corbett
Activities by David Bell, Pie Corbett
Geoff Leyland and Mick Seller

Illustrations by Diann Timms

This morning the postman brought a parcel.

How many faces can you see on the parcel?
Does it have any faces that you can't see?
The parcel is a cuboid shape.
Can you find any other cuboid shapes at home?
Count the number of faces.

'It's for Dad. Better not touch,' said Mum.

Talk about how you would find out what was in the box.
Find a small box or a plastic container with a lid. Put something inside it.
Ask someone to shake the box and to try to guess what is inside.
Now ask them to do the same for you. When you are trying to guess what's in the box, think about whether it's heavy or light, hard or soft, one item or several.

Jenny told Baby not to touch the parcel.

Does the shape of a parcel give you any clues about what's inside?
Play 'guess what's in the parcel' with some friends.
Wrap up a toy in lots of layers of paper.
Sit in a circle with your friends and ask Mum or Dad to play some music.
Every time the music stops, the person holding the parcel tries to guess what's inside before taking off one layer of paper.
See how many people can guess what the toy is before the last piece of paper is unwrapped.

But Baby did.

What sorts of things are you not allowed to touch?

Do you like getting parcels?

Make up a pretend parcel with Mum or Dad's help.
You will need something to put inside it, wrapping paper and sticky tape.
Write the address on the parcel.

Guess what was inside.

Guess what is inside the parcel.

Make a feely box by hiding some objects inside a box. Blindfold a friend, then ask them to feel inside the box and guess what the objects are.

Try describing the objects to your friend before you say what they are.

Was it the chimps taking their tea?

Does each chimp have their own cup and saucer?
Point to the cup and saucer of each chimp.
What about a plate?
Who doesn't have a plate?

Was it a whale
swimming in the sea?

Take a piece of newspaper and cut out some different-sized whale shapes.

Try to fan them across the floor using an old magazine. It might be easier if you curl up the whales a little bit.

Talk about what is making them move, and how real whales and fish move in the sea.

Was it a sausage taking a chance?

Do you ever eat sausages?
How long are they?
Are they longer than a loaf of bread?
Are they shorter than a Swiss roll?
Try to draw a picture of all the foods that you know that are longer and shorter than a sausage.

Was it a pig
doing a dance?

Was it a star
burning the packet?

Look at the shape of the star.
How many points has it?
How many edges does it have?
Do you know any shapes which have four sides?
What do you call a shape which has three sides?

Was it a temper making a racket?

Are you ever in a bad mood? Who in your family gets into moods? Draw some faces that look cross. Ask Mum or Dad to write in what they are saying, and what has happened to make them so cross. You could make up a story about your cross people.

'Stop!' shouted Baby, closing the box tight.

Try to remember all the things that might have been in the box.

What can you see behind the box?

What is in front of the box?

What you do think will come out of the box?

Baby fixed that parcel with a stare...

Try playing the game where you stare at a friend for as long as you can before one of you starts laughing. Then try telling each other jokes or funny stories to see who can keep a straight face the longest.

...and put it back, carefully.

Baby put the parcel back carefully.
How careful can you be?
Put some strips of paper, curled into circles, on to a tray.
Using a spoon, pick them up one at a time and put them into a box.
Can you pick them up two at a time?
Now try picking them up with one eye closed and then with two eyes closed.

When Dad came home
and opened the parcel...

Try playing a game of magic boxes with a friend.
Pretend that you each have a magic box that no-one else can see.
Try to guess what is in each other's box by asking lots of questions.
You could pretend to open your magic box and take out the contents to use or play with.

Activity Notes

Pages 2-3 Two- and three-dimensional shapes have a number of characteristics which young children can begin to identify. Get them to count the number of faces that can be seen. This can be repeated with other shapes around the house.

Pages 4-5 By shaking and listening, children will have ideas and can make guesses. Ask them to explain the reasons behind their guesses, eg 'Do you think it's hard... soft... round... square?' etc.
Try also placing a few familiar objects in a pillow case. Attempt to identify the objects by feeling them from the outside. Again, ask why certain guesses are made.

Pages 6-7 The sense of touch becomes more refined as the range of experiences of a young child increases. To develop the activity, wrap up some familiar objects in a piece of material so that their outline can be clearly seen. Guess what each is without touching the parcel.

Pages 8-9 Young children enjoy the excitement of sending and receiving parcels. When visiting friends or relatives, they could wrap up a small gift - even just a biscuit - and pretend to write an address on the parcel. Children also enjoy being lifted up to push letters into the postbox. Involvement with sending and receiving letters and cards teaches children about how writing can be used to send messages.

Pages 10-11 Children love guessing games. Encourage your child to describe what each object feels like - its shape, size and texture. This helps to develop sensory discrimination and use of language.

Pages 12-13 Children need to be able to match up pairs of related objects such as knives and forks and cups and saucers. This helps them to identify connections and establish relationships.

Pages 14-15 In order to make an object move, a force must be applied. In this instance, the movement of air should be sufficient to move the whales! As an extension, take a toilet roll tube and cut it into different sized rings. Which of these move the furthest when fanned by a magazine? Consider why some move more than others.

Pages 16-17 The language of comparison such as 'shorter than', 'longer than', etc is the beginning of an understanding of measurement. It is better if such comparisons are of nearly similar sized objects so that these are not extreme comparisons.

Pages 18-19 Copying a beat and discriminating between different rhythms require careful listening and co-ordination. The development of these skills is very important for pre-school children. Extend this idea by combining clapping with marching in time. Follow this by marching and swinging arms in time to a beat.

Pages 20-21 The characteristics of two- and three-dimensional shapes such as faces, points and edges can be explored by young children. Encourage them to use this language in an effort to develop more precise mathematical vocabulary.

Pages 22-23 Learning to read each other's moods and being able to respond accordingly is an important skill. You could follow this activity by drawing a list of pictures together showing things that make you happy.

Pages 24-25 Positional language is often picked up naturally by young children. Reinforce this by giving instructions using phrases such as 'in front of', 'behind' or 'above and below' when children are carrying out practical tasks.

Pages 26-27 Young children usually find funny faces and slapstick amusing. As their language develops, they begin to enjoy jokes that involve word play. Read rhymes and poetry with your child to help them develop a love of words and their sounds.

Pages 28-29 A steady hand and good hand-eye co-ordination are needed to move the objects slowly and carefully. Develop this activity by using a drinking straw to pick up the paper curls. Repeat, using the other hand. Talk about which hand was the most successful and why you think this was.

Pages 30-31 This is an imaginative guessing game. If the box is magic, there could be anything inside it - like Dr Who's Tardis, the inside could be larger than the outside. You might have an elephant in the box, or a supermarket, or an exploding teapot, or a teddy that sings.... The crazier it gets, the more fun it is creating something new.